A Picture Book of Abraham Lincoln

David A. Adler

illustrated by John & Alexandra Wallner

A TRUMPET CLUB SPECIAL EDITION

Published by The Trumpet Club
666 Fifth Avenue, New York, New York 10103

ISBN: 0-440-84746-X

This edition published by arrangement with
Holiday House, Inc.
Printed in the United States of America
January 1991

10 9 8 7 6 5 4 3 2
UPC

For GABRIELLA GOLDWYN

D.A.

Many thanks to KATE, JOHN and MARGERY.

J.W. and A.W.

ABRAHAM LINCOLN was born on February 12, 1809 in a one-room log cabin in Kentucky.

Abraham and his older sister Sarah helped in the house and on the farm. When they were not needed at home, they walked two miles to school and two miles back.

When Abraham was seven years old his family moved farther west, to Indiana. Abraham helped his father chop down trees. They cleared the land for their farm and built a new log cabin.

When Abraham was nine his mother died. A year later his father married Sarah Bush Johnston, a widow with three children. Abraham's new stepmother was good to Abraham. He called her "my angel mother."

Abraham loved books. Sometimes he walked many miles to borrow one. When he plowed the fields he often stopped to read.

In 1830, when Abraham was twenty-one, his family moved to Illinois. Abraham helped his father plant corn and build a fence and a new house.

Abraham was tall and thin. He was also very strong. In 1831 he and two other men built a flatboat. They floated it down the Mississippi River to New Orleans.

In New Orleans Abraham saw a slave market for the first time. Black slaves in chains were being sold like cattle. Seeing that done to people made Abraham miserable. He never forgot what he saw.

Abraham took a steamboat up the river to New Salem, Illinois where he worked as a clerk in a general store. He was twenty-two years old. Abraham laughed, told jokes and stories and loved to talk about politics. People liked him.

In 1834 Abraham Lincoln began to study law. Two years later he became a lawyer and moved to Springfield, the new capital of Illinois.

Abraham ran for public office many times. He served in the Illinois legislature. For two years he was also a member of the United States House of Representatives.

In Springfield Abraham fell in love with Mary Todd. She was lively and smart. They were married in 1842.

They had four sons, Robert, Edward, William and Thomas.

In 1858 Abraham was chosen by the new Republican party to run for the United States Senate. He ran against Senator Stephen A. Douglas.

Abraham Lincoln spoke out against slavery. He and Senator Douglas had many debates. Lincoln lost the election, but the debates made him famous throughout the country.

In 1860 Abraham Lincoln ran against Senator Stephen A. Douglas for president of the United States. This time Abraham Lincoln was elected.

When Abraham Lincoln became president there were more than three million black slaves in the southern states. Voters in the South were not happy to have a president who hated slavery.

Soon after Abraham Lincoln was elected president eleven southern states withdrew from the United States. They formed their own government, the Confederate States of America.

On April 12, 1861 Confederate soldiers fired on Fort Sumter, a United States fort in South Carolina. The war between the North and South, the Civil War, began.

Abraham Lincoln led the war to keep the country united.

During the war Lincoln wrote the Emancipation Proclamation. It declared that all slaves in the Confederate states were free.

In 1863 Lincoln spoke at Gettysburg, Pennsylvania. His speech became known as the Gettysburg Address. He said our government "of the people, by the people, for the people, shall not perish from the earth."

In 1864 the North won some important battles. Later that year Abraham Lincoln was re-elected president.

On April 9, 1865 the war ended. The South surrendered to the North. The war had lasted four years. Many had died.

Five days later, on the evening of April 14, Abraham and Mary Lincoln were at the theater. One hour after the play began there was a shot. John Wilkes Booth, an actor who favored the South, had shot the president. Lincoln died the next day.

A train carried Abraham Lincoln's body to Springfield, Illinois. Millions of Americans came to watch the train pass by, to say good-bye to Abraham Lincoln.

People called him "Honest Abe," "Father Abraham" and "Savior of the Union." Some say Abraham Lincoln was our greatest president.

IMPORTANT DATES

1809	Born on February 12 in Kentucky.
1818	Nancy Hanks Lincoln, Abraham's mother, died.
1842	Married Mary Todd on November 4.
1847–1849	Served as a member of the United States House of Representatives.
1858	Debated Senator Stephen A. Douglas in a losing campaign for United States Senate.
1860	Elected the sixteenth president of the United States.
1861	The first shots of the Civil War fired on April 12 at Fort Sumter, South Carolina.
1863	Issued Emancipation Proclamation on January 1 and delivered Gettysburg Address on November 19.
1865	Confederate forces surrendered on April 9. Civil War ended.
1865	President Abraham Lincoln shot on April 14. He died the next day.